Impressum
Verlag: BABADADA GmbH, Nedderfeld 112 , 22529 Hamburg
Geschäftsführer / Verlagsleitung: Harald Hof
Druck: Books on Demand GmbH, In de Tarpen 42, 22848 Norderstedt

Imprint
Publisher: BABADADA GmbH, Nedderfeld 112 , 22529 Hamburg, Germany
Managing Director / Publishing direction: Harald Hof
Print: Books on Demand GmbH, In de Tarpen 42, 22848 Norderstedt

# school

# xue xiao

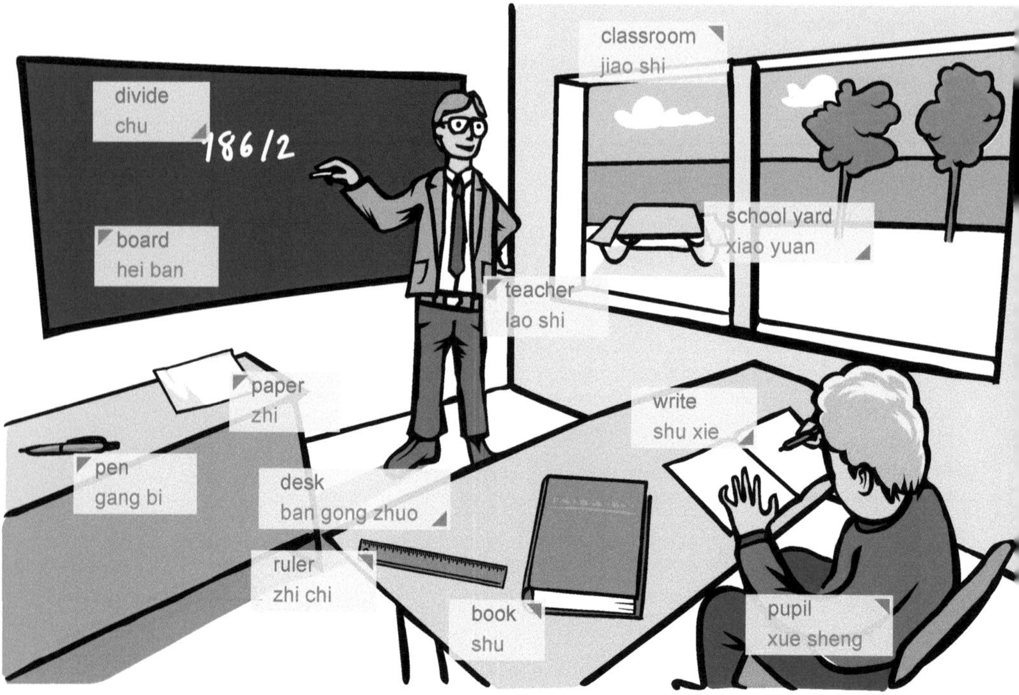
classroom
jiao shi
divide
chu
186/2
board
hei ban
school yard
xiao yuan
teacher
lao shi
paper
zhi
write
shu xie
pen
gang bi
desk
ban gong zhuo
ruler
zhi chi
book
shu
pupil
xue sheng

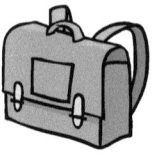

satchel

shu bao

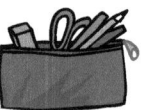

pencil case

qian bi he

pencil

qian bi

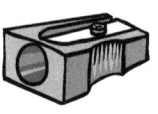

pencil sharpener

juan bi dao

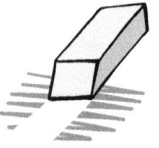

rubber

xiang pi ca

drawing pad

hua ban

drawing

tu hua

paintbrush

hua bi

paint box

yan liao he

scissors

jian dao

glue

jiao shui

exercise book

lian xi ce

homework

jia ting zuo ye

number

shu zi

add

jia

subtract

jian

multiply

cheng

calculate

ji suan

letter

zi mu

alphabet

zi mu biao

word

zi

text

ke wen

read

du

chalk

fen bi

lesson

shang ke

register

deng ji

examination

kao shi

certificate

zheng shu

school uniform

xiao fu

education

jiao yu

encyclopedia

bai ke quan shu

university

da xue

microscope

xian wei jing

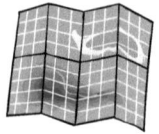

map

di tu

waste-paper basket

fei zhi kuang

# travel
# lü xing

hotel
jiu dian
Grand
hostel
qing nian lü xing she
currency exchange office
wai bi dui huan chu
car
qi che

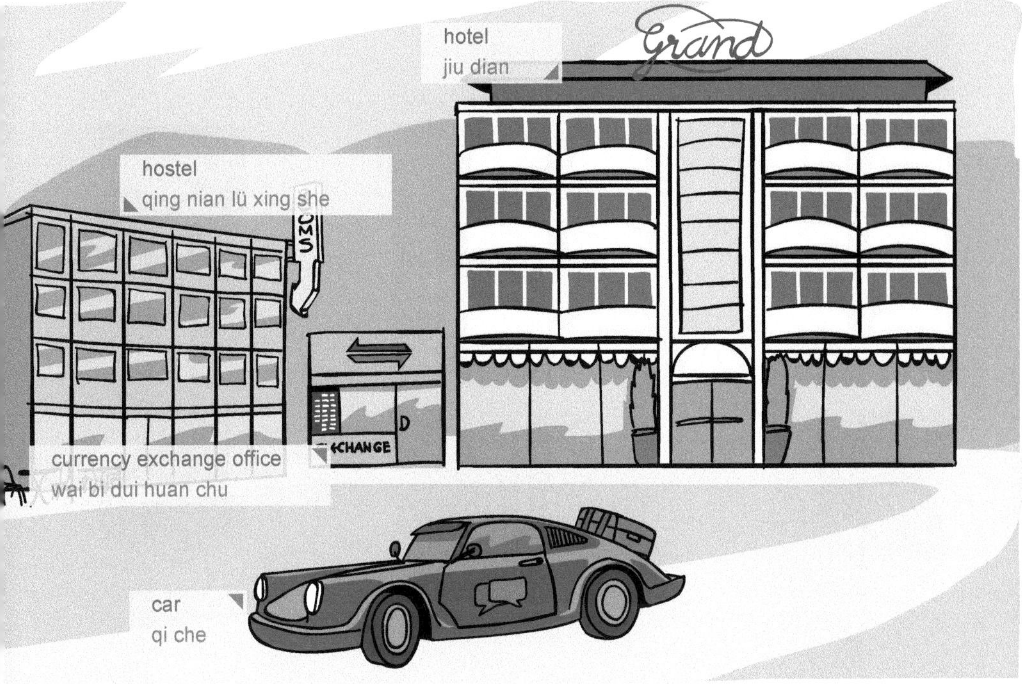

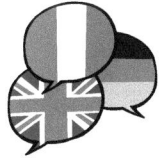

language

yu yan

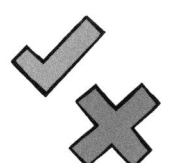

yes / no

shi/fou

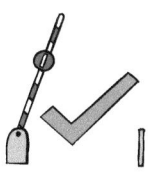

Okay

hao de

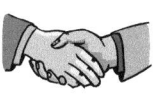

hello

nin hao

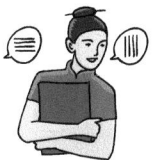

translator

fan yi yuan

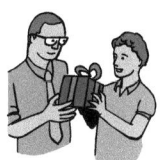

Thank you

xie xie

how much is...?

......duo shao qian?

I don´t get it

wo bu ming bai

problem

wen ti

Good evening!

wan shang hao!

Good morning!

zao shang hao!

Good night!

wan an!

goodbye

zai jian

direction

fang xiang

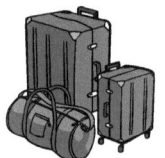

luggage

xing li

bag

bao

backpack

shuang jian bao

guest

ke ren

room

fang jian

sleeping bag

shui dai

tent

zhang peng

tourist information

lü you xin xi

beach

hai tan

credit card

xin yong ka

breakfast

zao can

lunch

wu can

dinner

wan can

Ticket

piao

elevator

dian ti

stamp

you piao

border

bian jie

customs

hai guan

embassy

da shi guan

visa

qian zheng

passport

hu zhao

# transport

## jiao tong yun shu

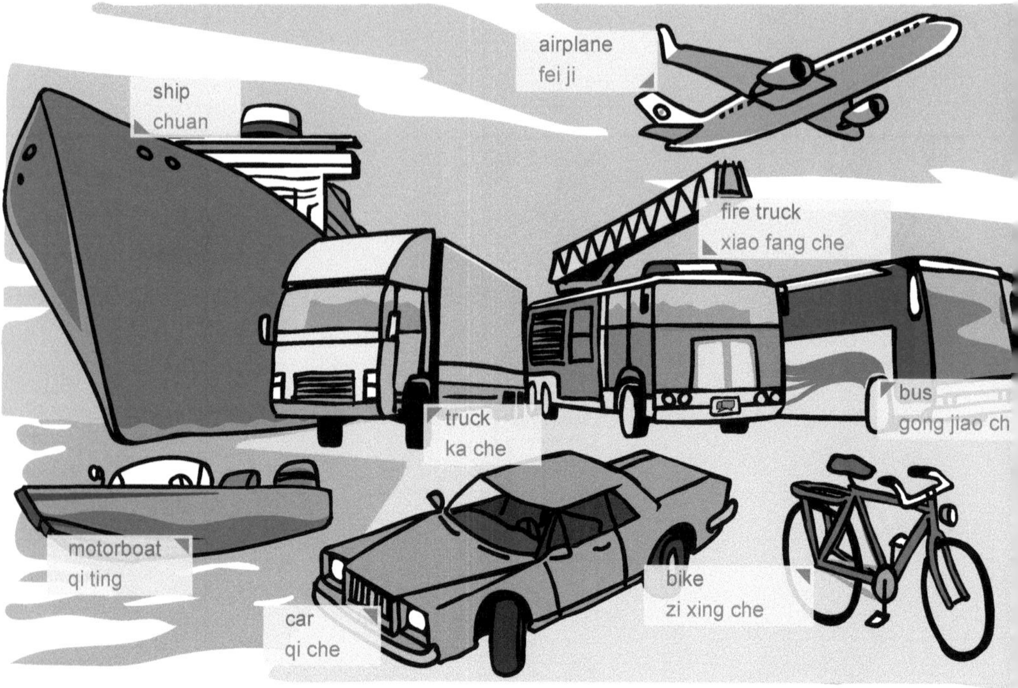

airplane
fei ji
ship
chuan
fire truck
xiao fang che
bus
gong jiao ch
truck
ka che
motorboat
qi ting
bike
zi xing che
car
qi che


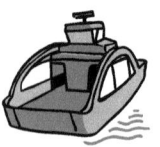

ferry

bai du chuan

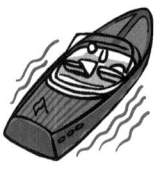

boat

xiao chuan

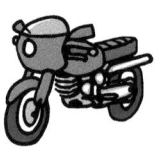

motorbike

mo tuo che

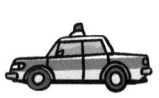

police car

jing che

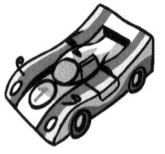

racing car

sai che

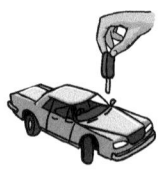

rental car

zu che

car sharing

pin che

tow truck

tuo che

garbage truck

la ji che

engine

fa dong ji

fuel

qi you

fuel station

jia you zhan

traffic sign

jiao tong biao zhi

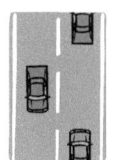

traffic

jiao tong

traffic jam

jiao tong du sai

parking lot

ting che chang

train station

huo che zhan

tracks

gui dao

train

huo che

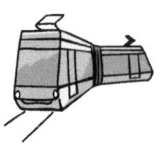

tram

dian che

wagon

huo che

helicopter

zhi sheng ji

airport

ji chang

tower

ta

passenger

cheng ke

container

ji zhuang xiang

carton

zhi ban xiang

cart

shou tui che

basket

lan zi

take off / land

qi fei/jiang luo

## city

## cheng shi

village

cun zhuang

city center

shi zhong xin

house

fang zi

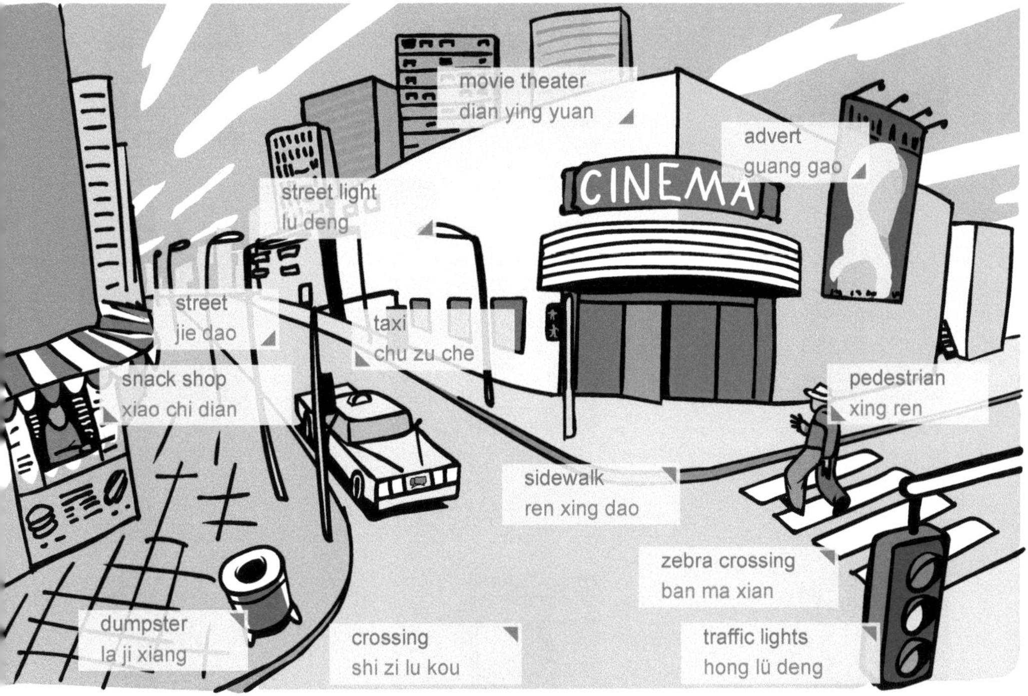

movie theater
dian ying yuan

advert
guang gao

street light
lu deng

street
jie dao

taxi
chu zu che

CINEMA

snack shop
xiao chi dian

pedestrian
xing ren

sidewalk
ren xing dao

zebra crossing
ban ma xian

dumpster
la ji xiang

crossing
shi zi lu kou

traffic lights
hong lü deng

hut

xiao wu

apartment

gong yu

train station

huo che zhan

city hall

shi zheng ting

museum

bo wu guan

school

xue xiao

university

da xue

bank

yin hang

hospital

yi yuan

hotel

jiu dian

pharmacy

yao fang

office

ban gong shi

book shop

shu dian

shop

shang dian

flower shop

hua dian

supermarket

chao shi

market

shi chang

department store

bai huo shang dian

fishmonger's shop

yu dian

mall

gou wu zhong xin

harbor

hai gang

park

gong yuan

bench

chang deng

bridge

qiao

stairs

lou ti

subway

di tie

tunnel

sui dao

bus stop

gong jiao che zhan

bar

jiu ba

restaurant

can guan

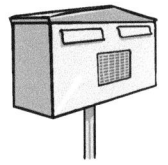

postbox

you tong

street sign

lu biao

parking meter

ting che ji shi qi

zoo

dong wu yuan

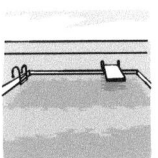

swimming pool

you yong guan

mosque

qing zhen si

farm

nong chang

pollution

wu ran

cemetery

mu di

church

jiao tang

playground

cao chang

temple

si miao

# landscape
## di xing

signpost
zhi shi pai

path
lu

meadow
cao di

stone
shi tou

tree
shu

hiker
tu bu lü xing zhe

river
he

grass
cao

flower
hua

valley

xia gu

hill

shan

lake

hu

forest

sen lin

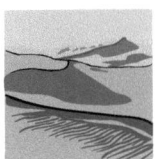

desert

sha mo

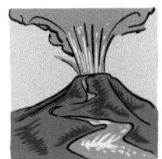

volcano

huo shan

castle

cheng bao

rainbow

cai hong

mushroom

mo gu

palm tree

zong lü shu

mosquito

wen zi

fly

cang ying

ant

ma yi

bee

mi feng

spider

zhi zhu

landscape - di xing

beetle

jia chong

frog

qing wa

squirrel

song shu

hedgehog

ci wei

hare

ye tu

owl

mao tou ying

bird

niao

swan

tian e

boar

ye zhu

deer

lu

moose

mi lu

dam

shui ba

wind turbine

feng li fa dian ji

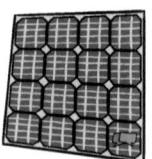

solar panel

tai yang neng dian chi ban

climate

qi hou

# restaurant
## can guan

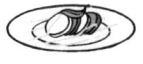

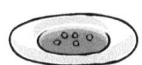

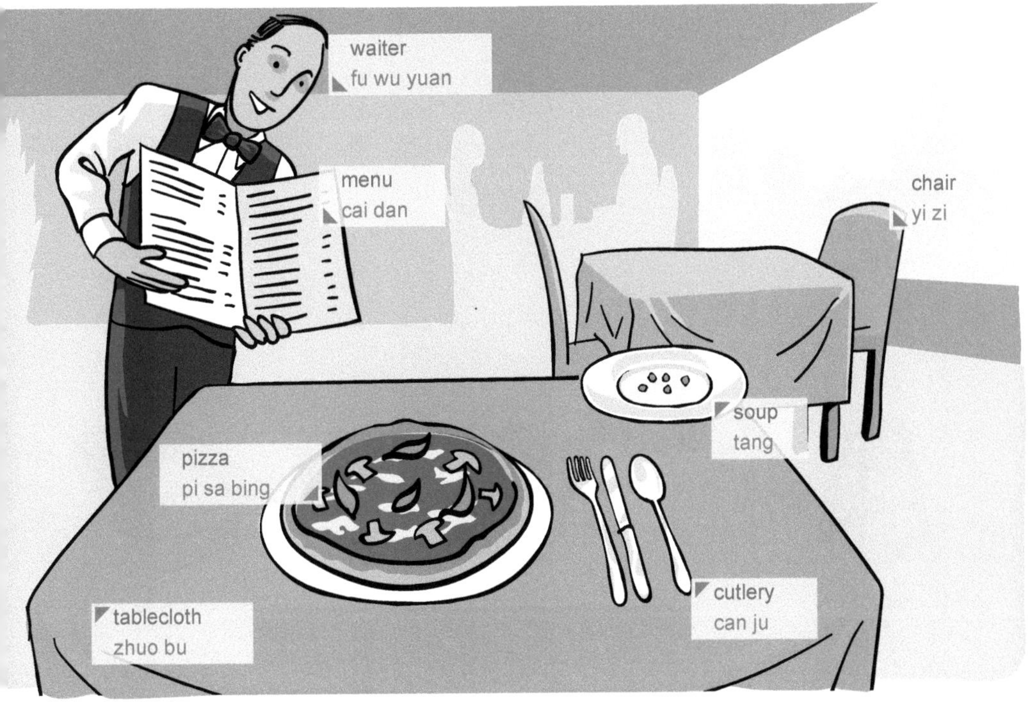

waiter
fu wu yuan
menu
cai dan
chair
yi zi
soup
tang
pizza
pi sa bing
cutlery
can ju
tablecloth
zhuo bu


starter
qian cai

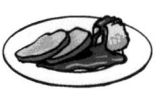

main course
zhu cai

dessert
tian dian

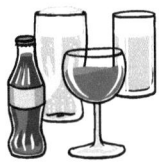

drinks
yin liao

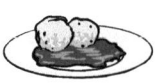

food
shi wu

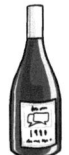

bottle
ping zi

fast food

kuai can

street food

jie bian xiao chi

teapot

cha hu

sugar bowl

tang he

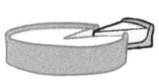

portion

yi fen fan cai

espresso machine

yi shi ka fei ji

high chair

gao jiao yi

bill

zhang dan

tray

tuo pan

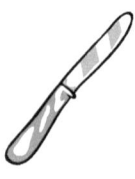

knife

dao

fork

can cha

spoon

shao zi

teaspoon

cha chi

serviette

can jin

glass

bo li bei

restaurant - can guan

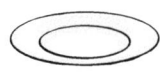

plate

die zi

soup plate

tang pan

saucer

die zi

sauce

jiang

salt shaker

yan ping

pepper mill

hu jiao mo

vinegar

cu

oil

shi yong you

spices

tiao wei liao

ketchup

fan qie jiang

mustard

jie mo

mayonnaise

dan huang jiang

# supermarket

## chao shi

special offer
te jia
FOR
customer
gu ke
dairy products
ru zhi pin
fruit
shui guo
shopping cart
gou wu che

BUTCHERS

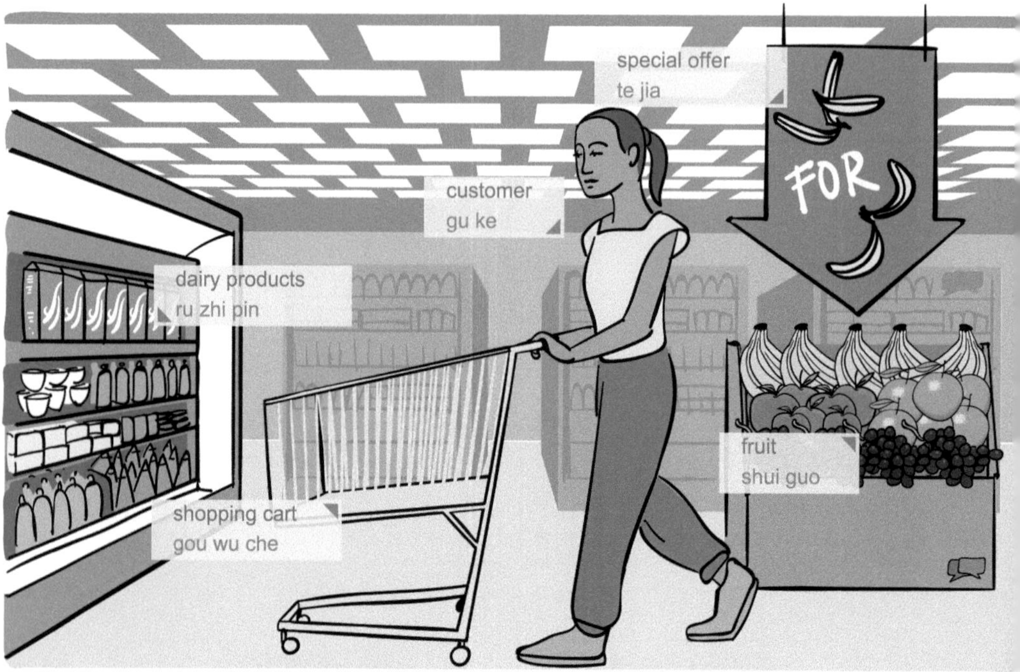

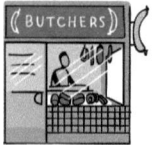

butcher's shop

rou pu

BAKERY

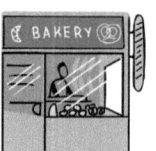

bakery

mian bao fang

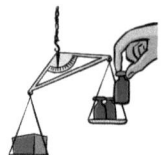

weigh

cheng zhong

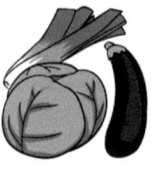

vegetables

shu cai

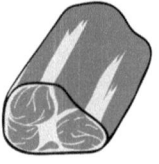

meat

rou

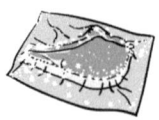

frozen food

leng dong shi pin

cold cuts

leng pan

canned food

guan tou shi pin

detergent

xi yi fen

candy

tian shi

household products

ri yong pin

cleaning products

qing jie yong pin

sales representative

xiao shou yuan

cash register

shou yin ji

cashier

shou yin yuan

shopping list

gou wu qing dan

opening hours

kai fang shi jian

wallet

qian bao

credit card

xin yong ka

bag

dai zi

plastic bag

su liao dai

water

shui

juice

guo zhi

milk

niu nai

coke

ke le

wine

hong jiu

beer

pi jiu

alcohol

jiu

cocoa

ke ke

tea

cha

coffee

ka fei

espresso

yi shi nong suo ka fei

cappuccino

ka bu qi nuo

banana

xiang jiao

apple

ping guo

orange

cheng zi

melon

xi gua

lemon

ning meng

carrot

hu luo bo

garlic

da suan

bamboo

zhu zi

onion

yang cong

mushroom

mo gu

nuts

jian guo

noodles

mian tiao

spaghetti

yi da li mian tiao

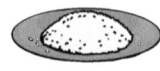

rice

mi fan

salad

sha la

fries

shu tiao

fried potatoes

zha tu dou

pizza

pi sa bing

hamburger

han bao bao

sandwich

san ming zhi

escalope

zha zhu pai

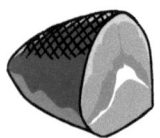

ham

huo tui

salami

sa la mi

sausage

xiang chang

chicken

ji rou

roast

kao rou

fish

yu

porridge oats

yan mai pian

muesli

mu zi li

cornflakes

yu mi pian

flour

mian fen

croissant

yang jiao mian bao

bread roll

mian bao juan

bread

mian bao

toast

kao mian bao

cookies

bing gan

butter

huang you

curd

ning ru

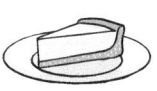

cake

dan gao

egg

dan

fried egg

jian dan

cheese

nai lao

ice cream

bing ji lin

sugar

tang

honey

feng mi

jelly

guo jiang

nougat cream

qiao ke li jiang

curry

ga li fan

# farm
# nong chang

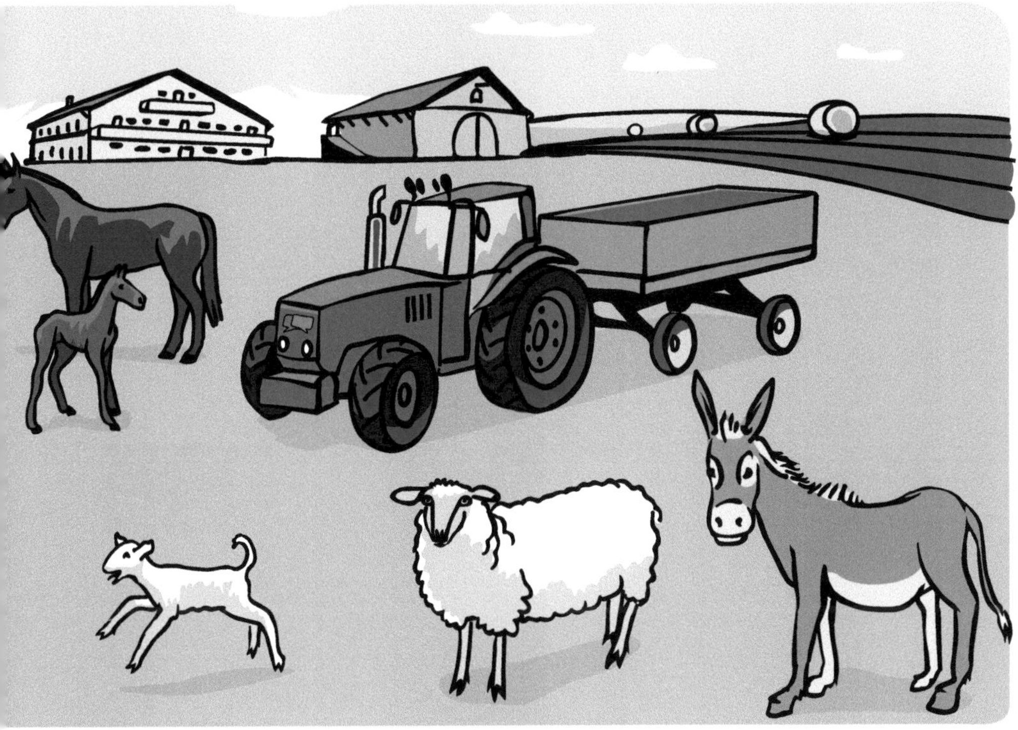

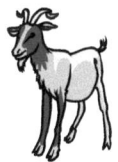

goat

shan yang

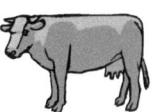

cow

nai niu

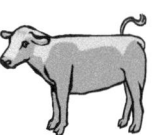

calf

niu du

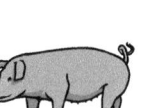

pig

zhu

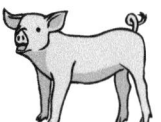

piglet

xiao zhu

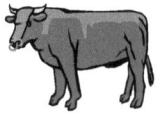

bull

gong niu

goose

e

duck

ya

chick

xiao ji

hen

mu ji

cockerel

gong ji

rat

shu

cat

mao

mouse

lao shu

ox

niu

dog

gou

dog house

gou wu

garden hose

hua yuan jiao shui ruan guan

watering can

sa shui hu

scythe

chang bing da lian dao

plow

li

sickle

lian dao

hoe

chu tou

pitchfork

chang bing cao pa

axe

fu tou

pushcart

du lun shou tui che

trough

si liao cao

milk can

niu nai guan

sack

ma bu dai

fence

zha lan

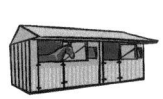

stable

ma jiu

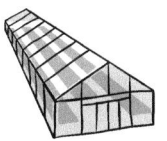

greenhouse

wen shi

soil

tu rang

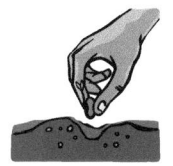

seed

zhong zi

fertilizer

fei liao

combine harvester

lian he shou ge ji

harvest

shou ge

harvest

shou ge

yams

shan yao

wheat

xiao mai

soya

da dou

potato

tu dou

corn

yu mi

rapeseed

you cai zi

fruit tree

guo shu

manioc

shu shu

grain

gu wu

# house
## fang zi

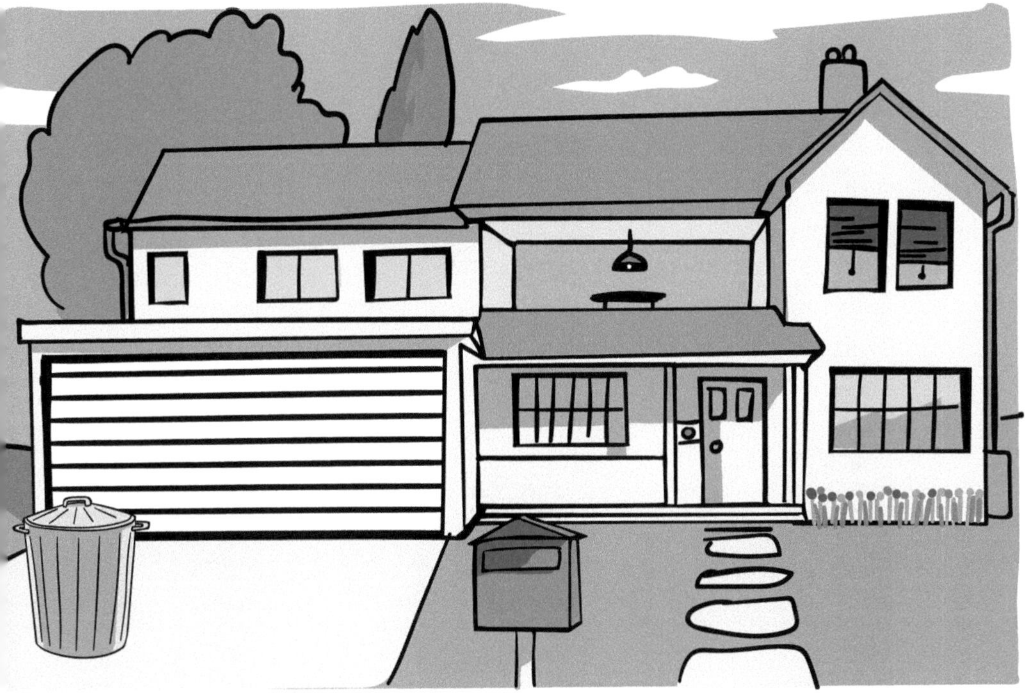

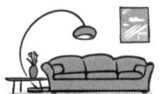

living room
ke ting

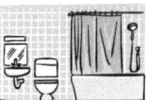

bathroom
yu shi

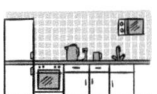

kitchen
chu fang

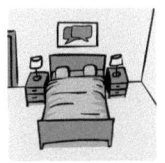

bedroom
wo shi

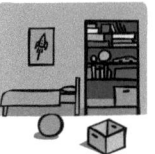

kids room
er tong fang

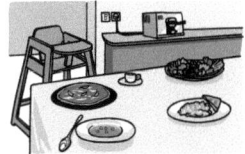

dining room
can ting

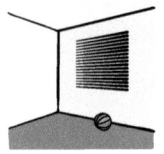

floor

di ban

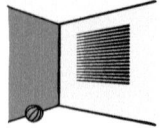

wall

qiang bi

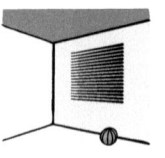

ceiling

diao ding

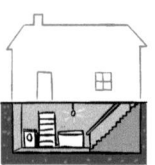

cellar

di jiao

sauna

sang na

balcony

yang tai

terrace

lu tai

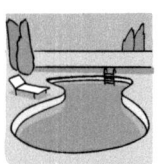

pool

you yong chi

lawn mower

ge cao ji

sheet

bei dan

bedspread

chuang zhao

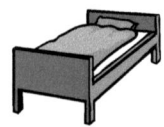

bed

chuang

broom

sao zhou

bucket

shui tong

switch

kai guan

# living room
# ke ting

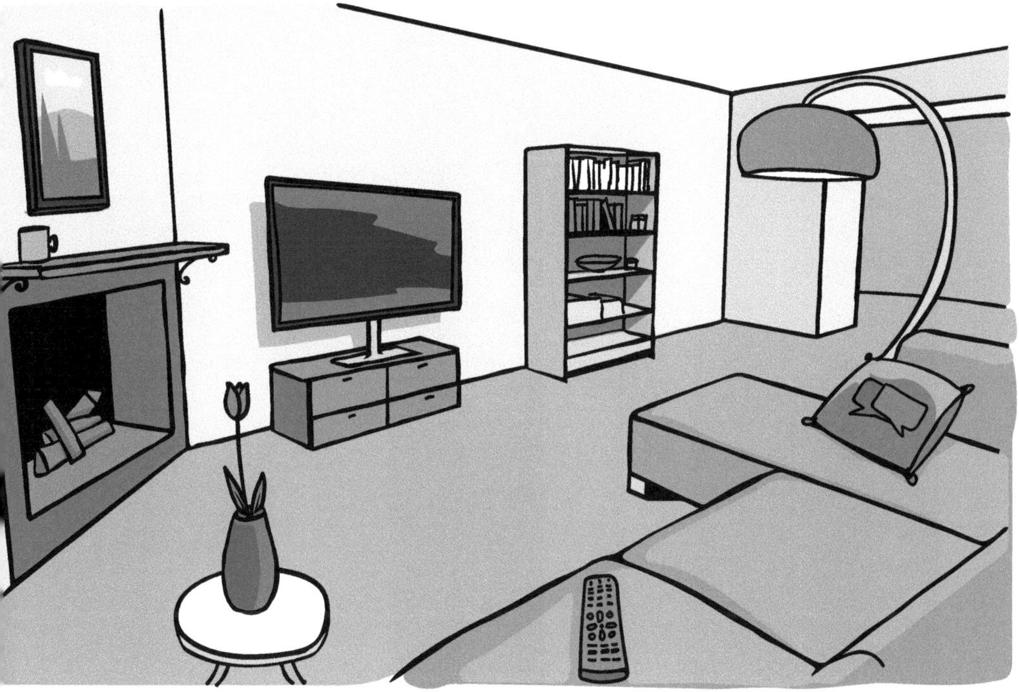

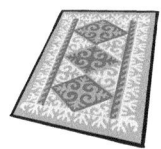

carpet

di tan

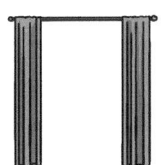

drape

chuang lian

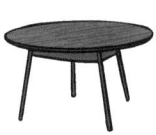

table

can zhuo

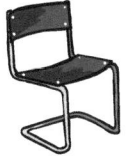

chair

yi zi

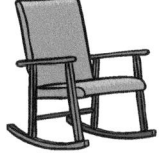

rocking chair

yao yi

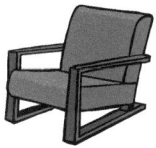

armchair

fu shou yi

book

shu

blanket

tan zi

decoration

zhuang shi pin

firewood

mu chai

film

dian ying

stereo system

gao bao zhen yin xiang

key

yao shi

newspaper

bao zhi

painting

you hua

poster

hai bao

radio

shou yin ji

notebook

bi ji ben

vacuum cleaner

xi chen qi

cactus

xian ren zhang

candle

la zhu

# kitchen
# chu fang

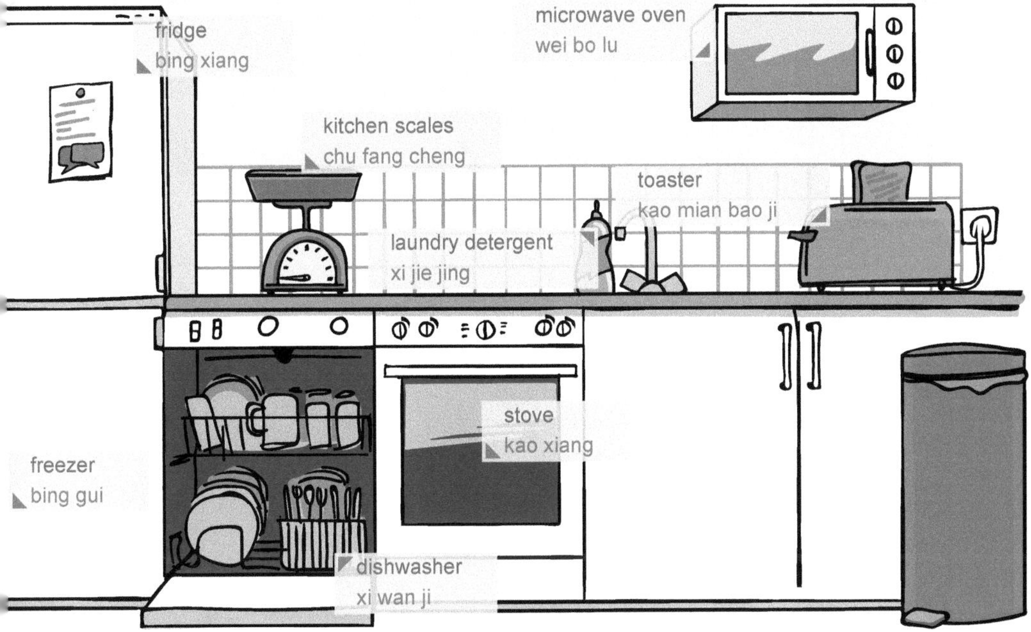

fridge
bing xiang
microwave oven
wei bo lu
kitchen scales
chu fang cheng
toaster
kao mian bao ji
laundry detergent
xi jie jing
stove
kao xiang
freezer
bing gui
dishwasher
xi wan ji


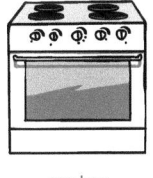

cooker

chui ju

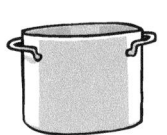

pot

guo

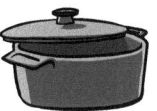

cast-iron pot

zhu tie guo

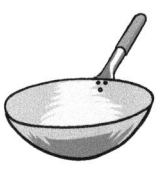

wok / kadai

sha guo

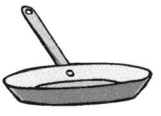

pan

ping di guo

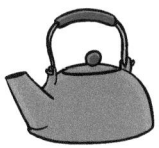

kettle

shui hu

**steamer**

zheng guo

**baking tray**

kao pan

**crockery**

tao ci guo

**mug**

ma ke bei

**bowl**

wan

**chopsticks**

kuai zi

**ladle**

chang bing shao

**spatula**

chan zi

**whisk**

jiao ban qi

**strainer**

lü wang

**sieve**

shai zi

**grater**

mo sui ji

**mortar**

yan bo

**barbecue**

shao kao

**fireplace**

ming huo

kitchen - chu fang

chopping board
cai ban

rolling pin
gan mian zhang

corkscrew
kai ping qi

can
guan zi

can opener
kai ping qi

oven cloth
ge re shou tao

sink
shui cao

brush
shua zi

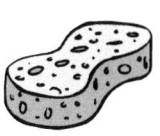

sponge
hai mian

blender
jiao ban ji

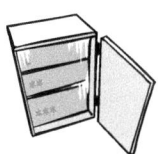

deep freezer
leng cang xiang

baby bottle
nai ping

tap
shui long tou

kitchen - chu fang

# bathroom
## yu shi

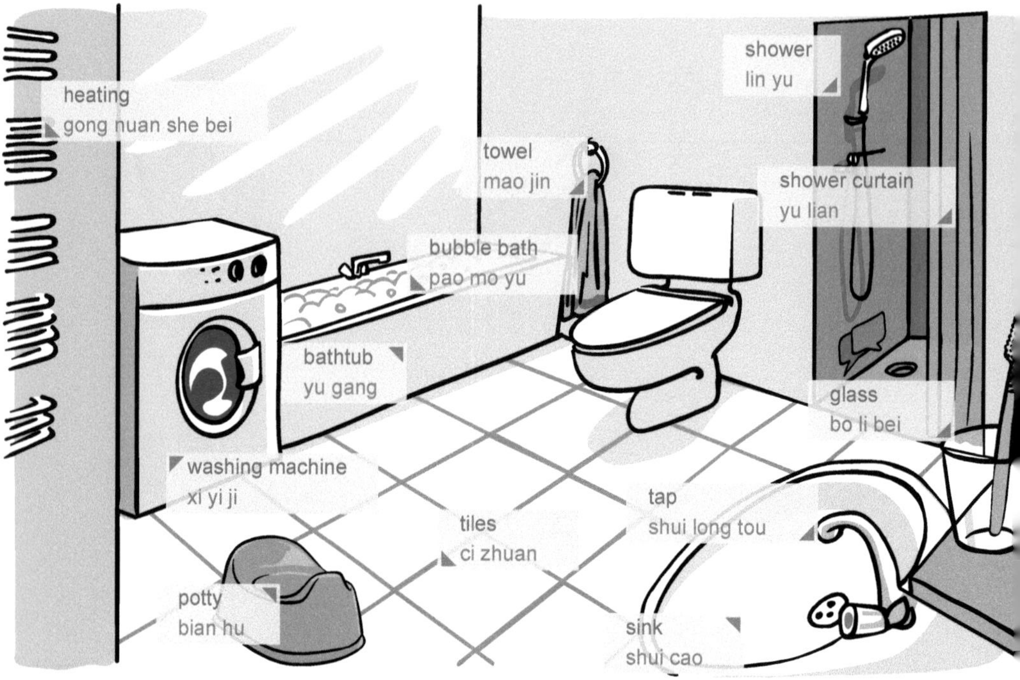

heating
gong nuan she bei

shower
lin yu

towel
mao jin

shower curtain
yu lian

bubble bath
pao mo yu

bathtub
yu gang

glass
bo li bei

washing machine
xi yi ji

tiles
ci zhuan

tap
shui long tou

potty
bian hu

sink
shui cao

toilet

ce suo

squat toilet

dun bian qi

bidet

zuo yu qi

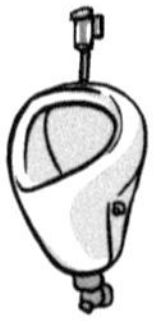

urinal

xiao bian chi

toilet paper

ce zhi

toilet brush

ma tong shua

toothbrush
ya shua

toothpaste
ya gao

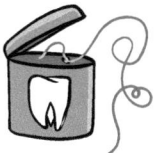

dental floss
ya xian

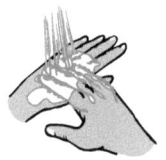

wash
xi

hand shower
shou chi shi pen lin tou

douche
chong xi qi

basin
xi lian pen

back brush
ca bei shua

soap
fei zao

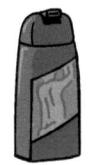

shower gel
mu yu lu

shampoo
xi fa shui

flannel
fa lan rong

drain
pai shui

creme
ru shuang

deodorant
chu chou ji

mirror

jing zi

hand mirror

shou jing

razor

ti xu dao

shaving foam

ti xu pao mo

aftershave

xu hou shui

comb

shu zi

brush

shua zi

hair-dryer

chui feng ji

hairspray

pen fa ding xing ji

makeup

hua zhuang pin

lipstick

chun gao

nail varnish

zhi jia you

cotton wool

hua zhuang mian

nail scissors

zhi jia jian

perfume

xiang shui

washbag

xi shu bao

stool

deng zi

weighing scales

ji zhong cheng

bathrobe

yu pao

rubber gloves

xiang jiao shou tao

tampon

wei sheng mian tiao

sanitary towel

wei sheng jin

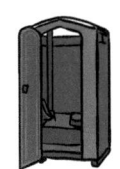

chemical toilet

hua xue ce suo

# kids room

# er tong fang

alarm clock
nao zhong
cuddly toy
mao rong wan ju
toy car
wan ju che
rattle
bo lang gu
doll's house
wan ju wu
present
li wu


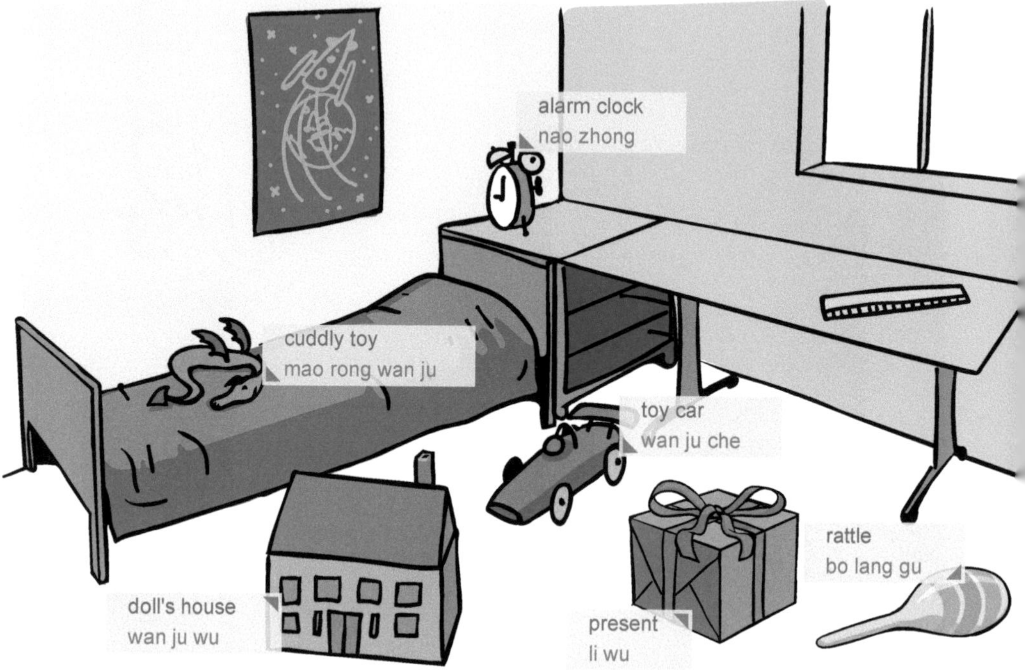

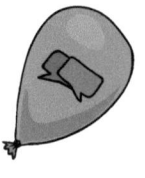

balloon

qi qiu

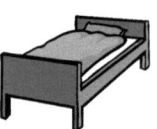

bed

chuang

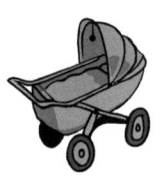

stroller

(yang wa wa yong)ying er che

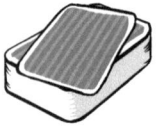

deck of cards

pu ke pai

jigsaw

pin tu

SUPER
MEGA


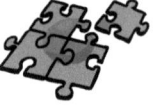

comic

man hua

lego bricks

le gao ji mu

toy blocks

ji mu wan ju

action figure

wan ju ren

romper suit

ying er fu

frisbee

fei pan

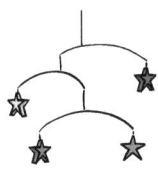

mobile

chuang ling wan ju

board game

qi pan you xi

dice

shai zi

model train set

huo che mo xing

pacifier

an fu nai zui

party

ju hui

picture book

hui ben

ball

qiu

doll

yang wa wa

play

wan

sandpit

sha keng

swing

qiu qian

toys

wan ju

video game console

you xi ji

tricycle

san lun che

teddy bear

tai di xiong

wardrobe

yi chu

# clothing
## yi fu

socks

wa zi

stockings

chang wa

tights

jin shen ku

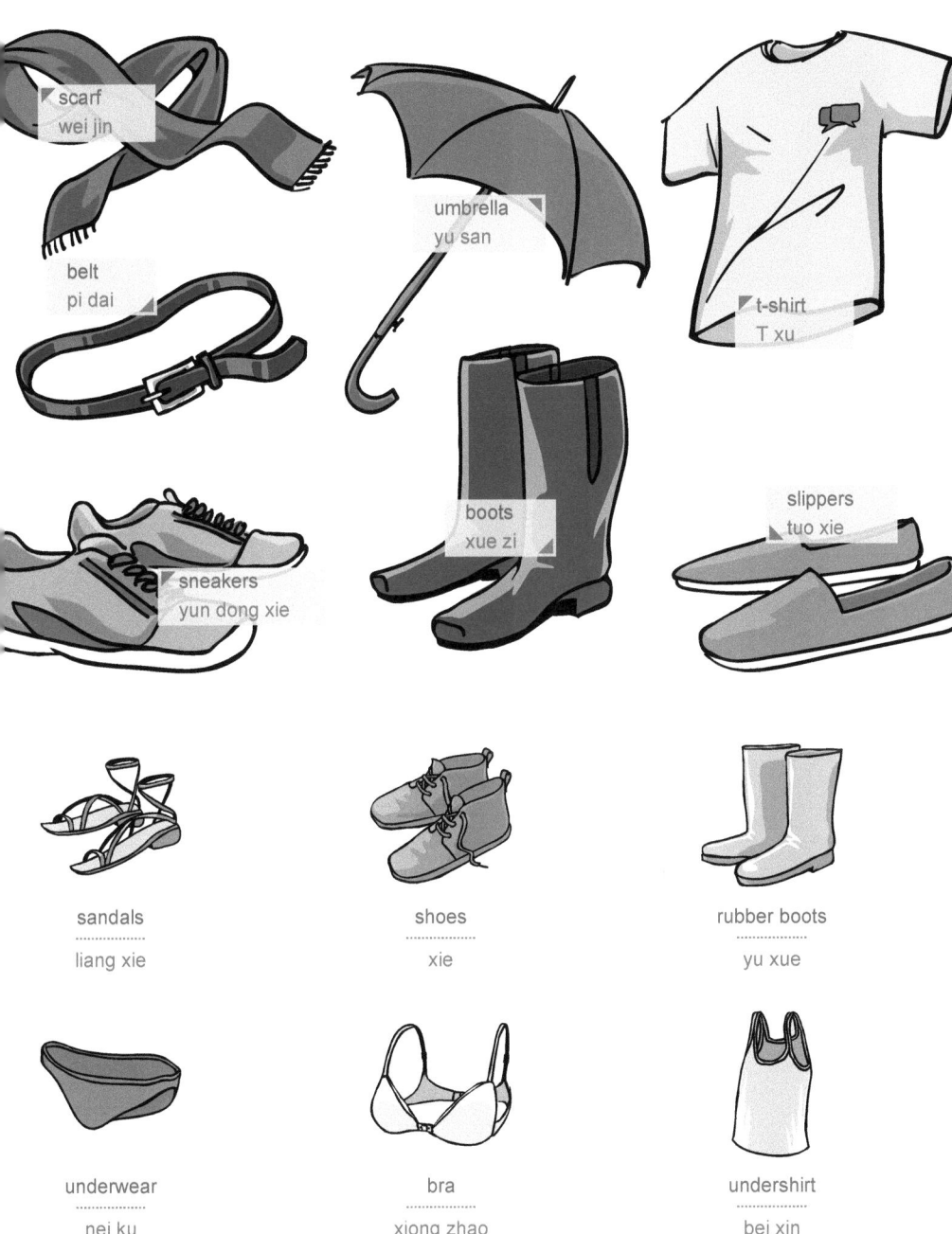

scarf
wei jin

umbrella
yu san

t-shirt
T xu

belt
pi dai

sneakers
yun dong xie

boots
xue zi

slippers
tuo xie

sandals
liang xie

shoes
xie

rubber boots
yu xue

underwear
nei ku

bra
xiong zhao

undershirt
bei xin

clothing - yi fu

body

shen ti

pants

ku zi

jeans

niu zai ku

skirt

duan qun

blouse

nü shi chen shan

shirt

chen shan

pullover

tao tou shan

sweater

wei yi

blazer

xi zhuang jia ke

jacket

jia ke

coat

wai tao

raincoat

yu yi

costume

tao zhuang

dress

lian yi qun

wedding dress

hun sha

suit

xi zhuang

nightgown

shui pao

pajamas

shui yi

sari

sha li

headscarf

tou jin

turban

bao tou jin

burka

bo ka

kaftan

ka fu tan

abaya

(a la bo shi)chang pao

swimsuit

yong yi

trunks

nan shi yong ku

shorts

duan ku

tracksuit

yun dong fu

apron

wei qun

gloves

shou tao

button

niu kou

glasses

yan jing

bracelet

shou lian

necklace

xiang lian

ring

jie zhi

earring

er huan

cap

bian mao

coat hanger

yi jia

hat

mao zi

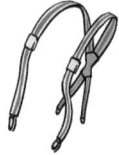

tie

ling dai

zip

la lian

helmet

tou kui

braces

bei dai

school uniform

xiao fu

uniform

zhi fu

bib
wei dou

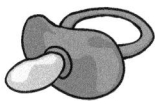

pacifier
an fu nai zui

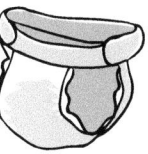

diaper
niao bu shi

# office
# ban gong shi

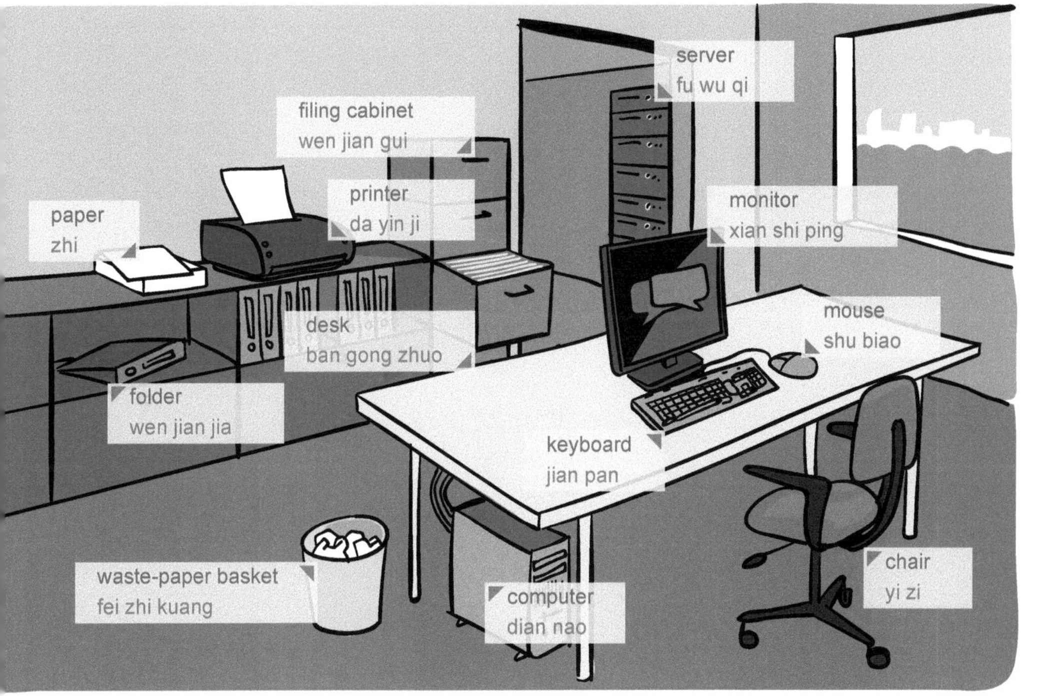

server
fu wu qi

filing cabinet
wen jian gui

printer
da yin ji

paper
zhi

monitor
xian shi ping

mouse
shu biao

desk
ban gong zhuo

folder
wen jian jia

keyboard
jian pan

waste-paper basket
fei zhi kuang

chair
yi zi

computer
dian nao

coffee mug
ka fei bei

calculator
ji suan qi

internet
yin te wang

laptop

bi ji ben dian nao

letter

xin jian

message

xiao xi

cell phone

shou ji

network

wang luo

photocopier

fu yin ji

software

ruan jian

telephone

dian hua

plug socket

cha zuo

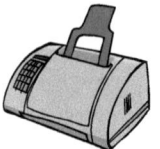

fax machine

chuan zhen ji

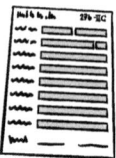

form

biao ge

document

wen jian

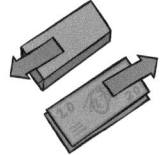

buy

mai

pay

fu qian

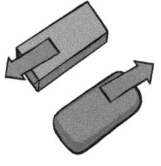

trade

jiao yi

money

xian jin

dollar

mei yuan

euro

ou yuan

yen

ri yuan

rouble

lu bu

Swiss franc

rui shi fa lang

renminbi yuan

ren min bi

rupee

lu bi

cash point

ti kuan chu

currency exchange office

wai bi dui huan chu

gold

jin

silver

yin

oil

shi you

energy

neng yuan

price

jia ge

contract

he tong

tax

shui jin

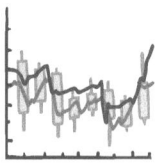

stock

gu piao

work

gong zuo

employee

zhi yuan

employer

lao ban

factory

gong chang

shop

shang dian

police officer
jing guan

fireman
xiao fang yuan

pilot
fei xing yuan

cook
chu shi

doctor
yi sheng

gardener

yuan ding

carpenter

mu jiang

seamstress

cai feng

judge

fa guan

chemist

hua xue jia

actor

yan yuan

bus driver

gong jiao che si ji

taxi driver

chu zu che si ji

fisherman

yu fu

cleaning lady

qing jie nü gong

roofer

wu ding gong

waiter

fu wu yuan

hunter

lie ren

painter

hua jia

baker

mian bao shi

electrician

dian gong

builder

jian zhu gong ren

engineer

gong cheng shi

butcher

tu fu

plumber

shui guan gong

postman

you di yuan

soldier

shi bing

architect

jian zhu shi

cashier

shou yin yuan

florist

hua nong

hairdresser

li fa shi

conductor

shou piao yuan

mechanic

ji xie shi

captain

chuan zhang

dentist

ya yi

scientist

ke xue jia

rabbi

la bi

imam

yi ma mu

monk

he shang

pastor

mu shi

# tools

# gong ju

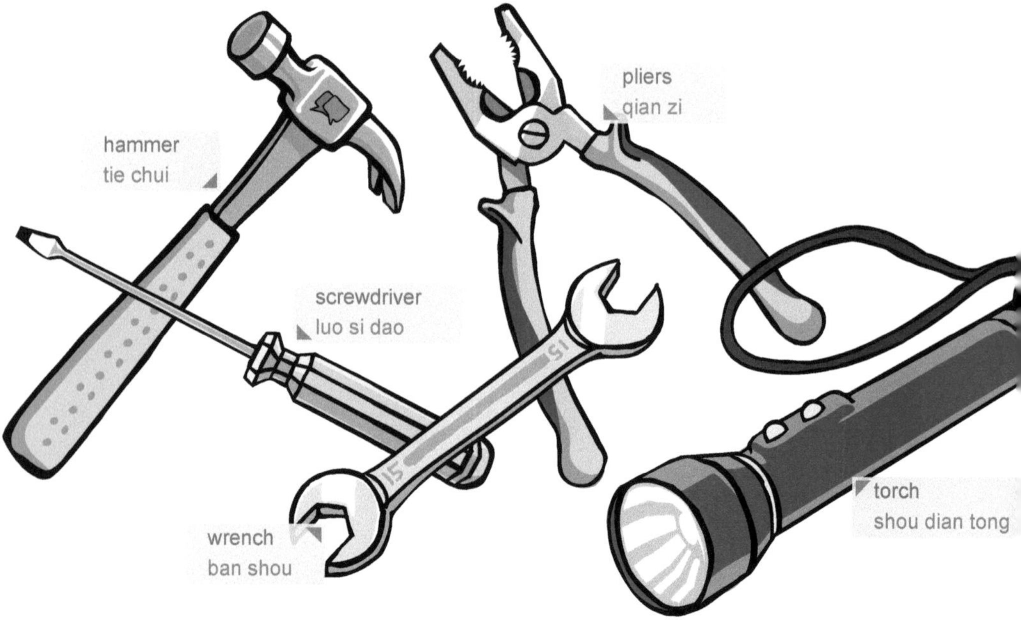

hammer
tie chui
pliers
qian zi
screwdriver
luo si dao
wrench
ban shou
torch
shou dian tong


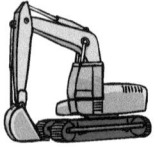

excavator

wa jue ji

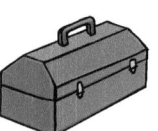

toolbox

gong ju xiang

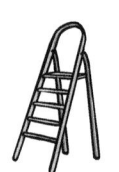

ladder

ti zi

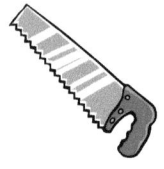

saw

ju zi

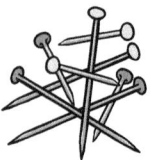

nails

ding zi

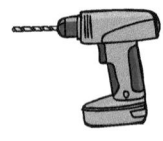

drill

zuan ji

repair

xiu

shovel

chan zi

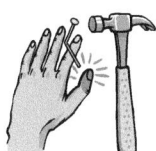

Damn!

kao!

dustpan

bo ji

paint can

you qi tong

screws

luo si

## musical instruments

## yue qi

loud speaker
yang sheng qi

drum set
da ji yue qi

guitar
ji ta

double bass
di yin ti qin

trumpet
xiao hao

piano

gang qin

violin

xiao ti qin

bass

bei si

timpani

ding yin gu

drums

gu

keyboard

dian zi qin

saxophone

sa ke si guan

flute

chang di

microphone

mai ke feng

# zoo
# dong wu yuan

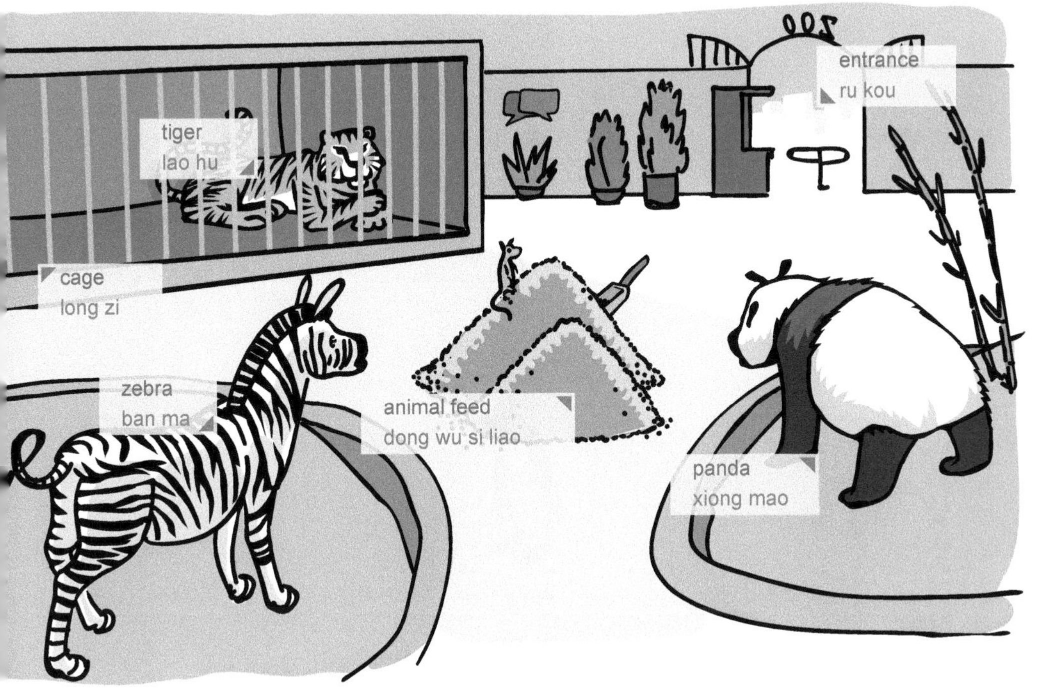

entrance
ru kou
tiger
lao hu
cage
long zi
zebra
ban ma
animal feed
dong wu si liao
panda
xiong mao


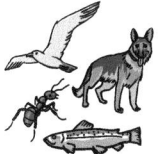

animals
dong wu

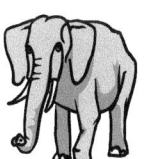

elephant
da xiang

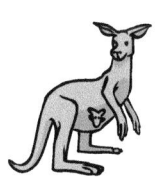

kangaroo
dai shu

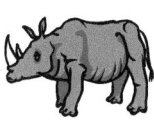

rhino
xi niu

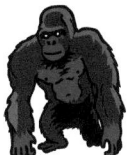

gorilla
da xing xing

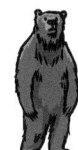

bear
xiong

camel

luo tuo

ostrich

tuo niao

lion

shi zi

monkey

hou zi

flamingo

huo lie niao

parrot

ying wu

polar bear

bei ji xiong

penguin

qi e

shark

sha yu

peacock

kong que

snake

she

crocodile

e yu

zookeeper

dong wu yuan guan li yuan

seal

hai bao

jaguar

mei zhou bao

pony

ai zhong ma

leopard

bao

hippo

he ma

giraffe

chang jing lu

eagle

lao ying

boar

ye zhu

fish

yu

turtle

gui

walrus

hai xiang

fox

hu li

gazelle

ling yang

American football
gan lan qiu

cycling
qi zi xing che

tennis
wang qiu

basketball
lan qiu

swimming
you yong

boxing
quan ji

ice hockey
bing qiu

soccer
ying shi zu qiu

badminton
yu mao qiu

athletics
tian jing

handball
shou qiu

skiing
hua xue

polo
ma qiu

laugh
xiao

jump
tiao

hug
yong bao

walk
zou lu

sing
chang

dream
zuo meng

pray
qi dao

kiss
qin wen

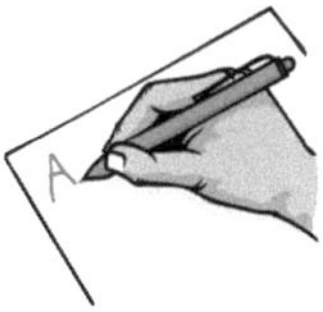

write
shu xie

draw
hua

show
zhan shi

push
tui

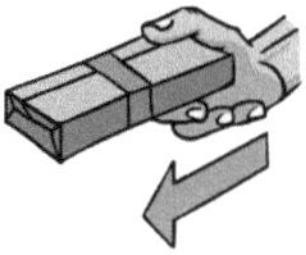

give
gei

take
na

activities - huo dong

63

have
you

do
zuo

be
dang

stand
zhan

run
pao

pull
la

throw
reng

fall
shuai dao

lie
tang

wait
deng dai

carry
xie dai

sit
zuo

get dressed
chuan yi

sleep
shui jiao

wake up
xing lai

look at

kan

cry

ku

stroke

fu mo

comb

shu tou

talk

jiao tan

understand

ming bai

ask

wen

listen

ting

drink

he

eat

chi

tidy up

qing li

love

ai

cook

zuo fan

drive

kai che

fly

fei

activities - huo dong          65

sail

hang xing

calculate

ji suan

read

du

learn

xue xi

work

gong zuo

marry

jie hun

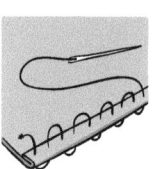

sew

feng

brush teeth

shua ya

kill

sha

smoke

chou yan

send

ji

# family
# jia

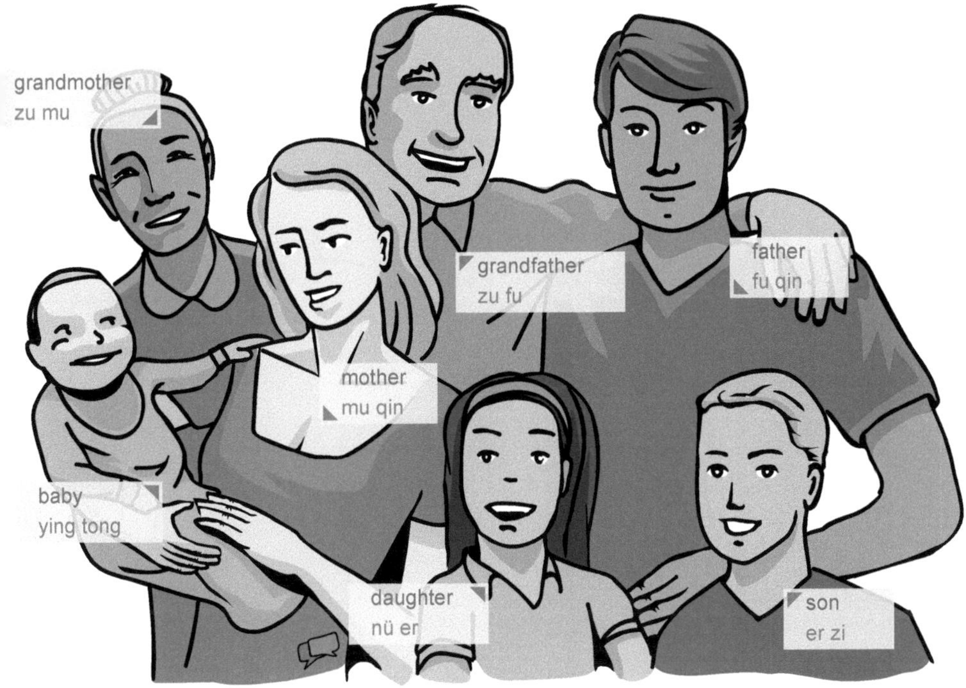
grandmother
zu mu
grandfather
zu fu
father
fu qin
mother
mu qin
baby
ying tong
daughter
nü er
son
er zi

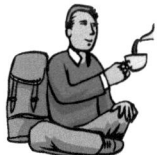

guest

ke ren

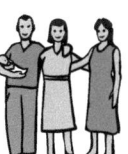

aunt

a yi

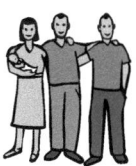

uncle

shu shu

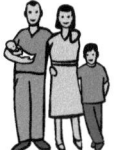

brother

xiong di

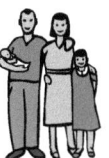

sister

jie mei

# body

# shen ti

forehead
qian e
eye
yan jing
shoulder
jian bang
finger
shou zhi
face
lian
chin
xia ba
hand
shou
leg
tui
breast
ru fang
arm
shou bi

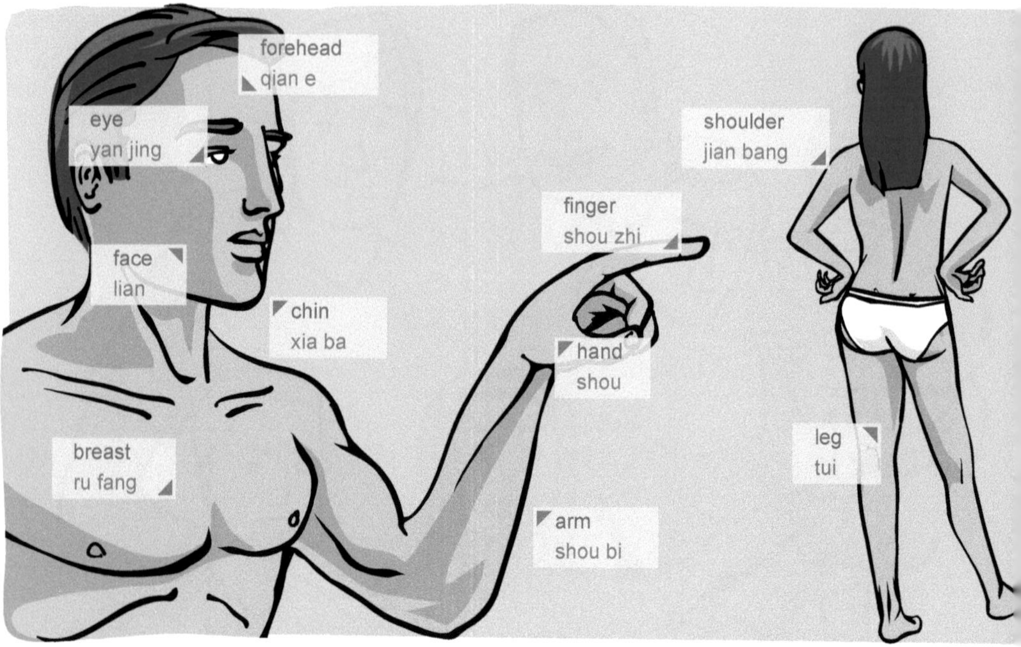

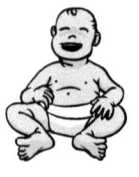

baby

ying tong

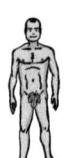

man

nan ren

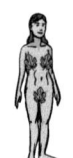

woman

nü ren

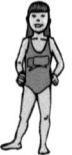

girl

nü hai

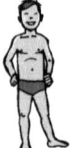

boy

nan hai

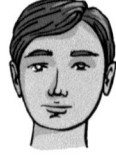

head

tou

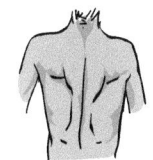

back

bei bu

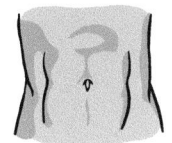

belly

du zi

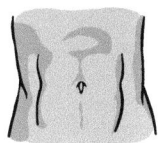

navel

du qi

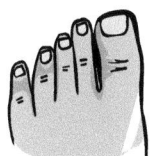

toe

jiao zhi

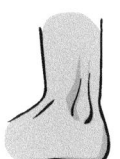

heel

jiao hou gen

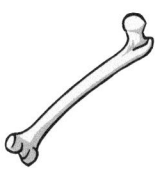

bone

gu tou

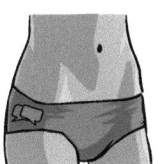

hip

tun bu

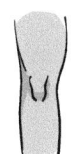

knee

xi gai

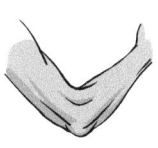

elbow

shou zhou

nose

bi zi

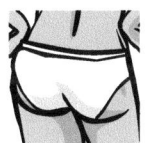

buttocks

pi gu

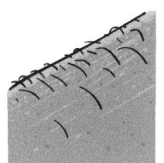

skin

pi fu

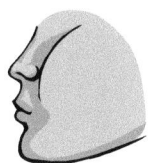

cheek

lian jia

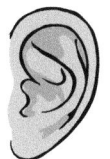

ear

er duo

lip

zui chun

mouth

zui

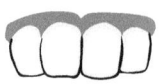

tooth

ya chi

tongue

she tou

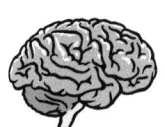

brain

nao

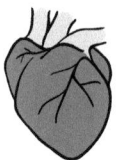

heart

xin zang

muscle

ji rou

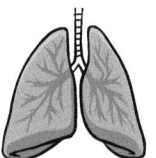

lung

fei

liver

gan zang

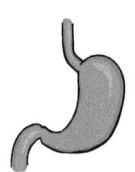

stomach

wei

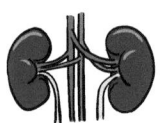

kidneys

shen zang

sex

xing jiao

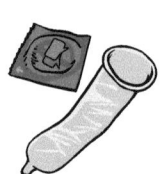

condom

bi yun tao

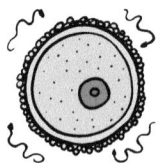

ovum

luan zi

semen

jing zi

pregnancy

huai yun

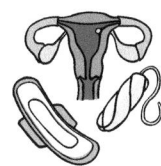

menstruation

yue jing

vagina

yin dao

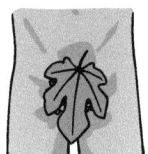

penis

yin jing

eyebrow

mei mao

hair

tou fa

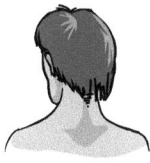

neck

bo zi

# hospital

## yi yuan

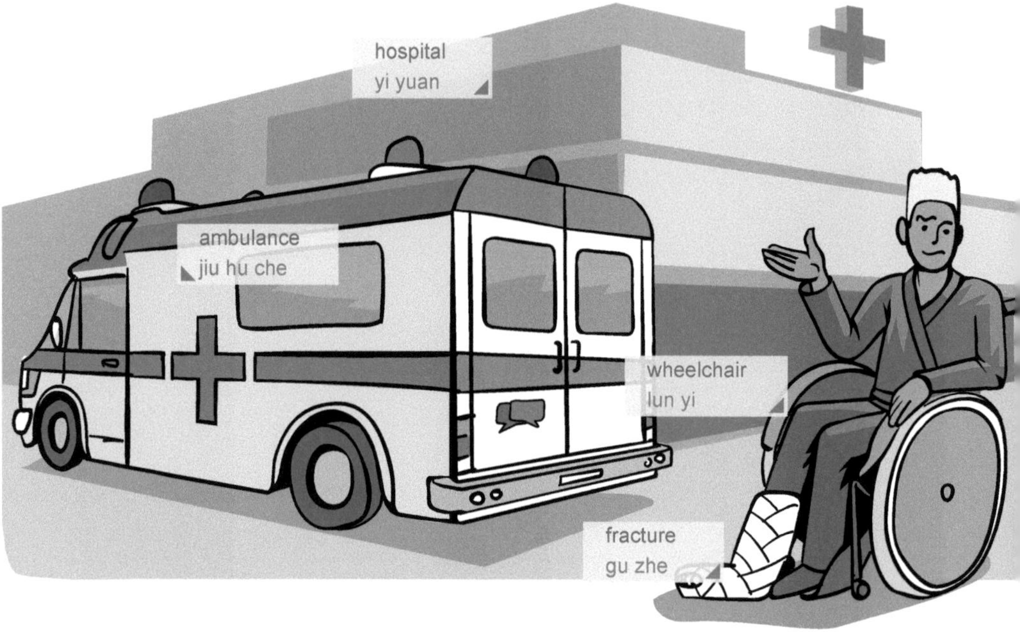

hospital
yi yuan
ambulance
jiu hu che
wheelchair
lun yi
fracture
gu zhe


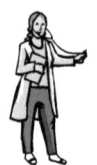

doctor

yi sheng

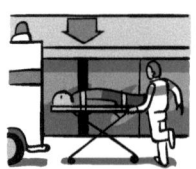

emergency room

ji zhen shi

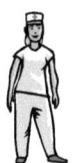

nurse

hu shi

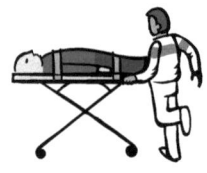

emergency

jin ji qing kuang

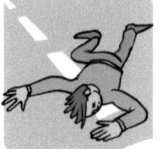

unconscious

hun mi

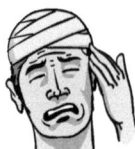

pain

tong

injury

shou shang

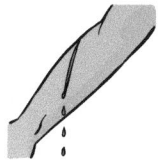

bleeding

chu xue

heart attack

xin zang bing fa zuo

stroke

zhong feng

allergy

guo min

cough

ke sou

fever

fa shao

flu

liu gan

diarrhea

fu xie

headache

tou tong

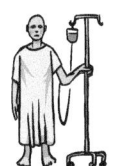

cancer

ai zheng

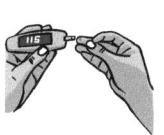

diabetes

tang niao bing

surgeon

wai ke yi sheng

scalpel

shou shu dao

operation

shou shu

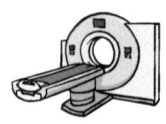

CT

CT

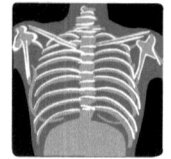

x-ray

X guang

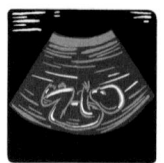

ultrasound

chao sheng bo

face mask

kou zhao

disease

ji bing

waiting room

hou zhen shi

crutch

guai zhang

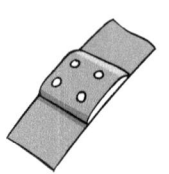

plaster

shi gao

bandage

beng dai

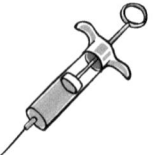

injection

zhu she

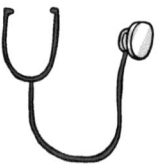

stethoscope

ting zhen qi

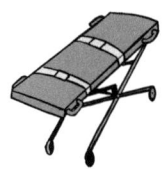

stretcher

dan jia

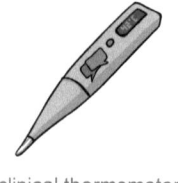

clinical thermometer

ti wen ji

birth

chu sheng

overweight

chao zhong

hearing aid

zhu ting qi

disinfectant

xiao du ye

infection

gan ran

virus

bing du

HIV / AIDS

ai zi bing

medicine

yao wu

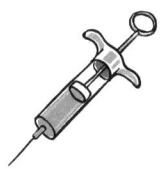

vaccination

jie zhong yi miao

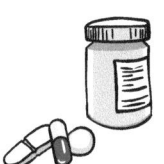

tablets

yao pian

pill

yao wan

emergency call

ji jiu dian hua

blood pressure monitor

xue ya ji

ill / healthy

sheng bing/jian kang

Help!

jiu ming!

alarm

jing bao

assault

tu ji

attack

gong ji

danger

wei xian

emergency exit

jin ji chu kou

Fire!

zhao huo la!

fire extinguisher

mie huo qi

accident

yi wai

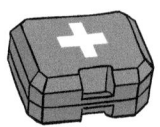

first-aid kit

ji jiu xiang

SOS

hu jiu xin hao

police

jing cha

Europe

ou zhou

North America

bei mei zhou

South America

nan mei zhou

Africa

fei zhou

Asia

ya zhou

Australia

ao zhou

Atlantic

da xi yang

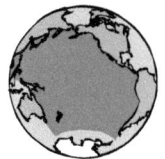

Pacific

tai ping yang

Indian Ocean

yin du yang

Antarctic Ocean

nan bing yang

Arctic Ocean

bei bing yang

North pole

bei ji

South pole

nan ji

Antarctica

nan ji zhou

earth

di qiu

land

lu di

sea

hai

island

dao

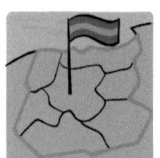

nation

guo jia

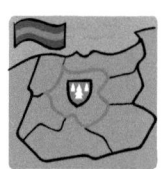

state

guo jia

clock face

zhong mian

hour hand

shi zhen

minute hand

fen zhen

second hand

miao zhen

What time is it?

xian zai ji dian?

day

tian

time

shi jian

now

xian zai

digital watch

dian zi biao

minute

fen

hour

shi

# week

## zhou

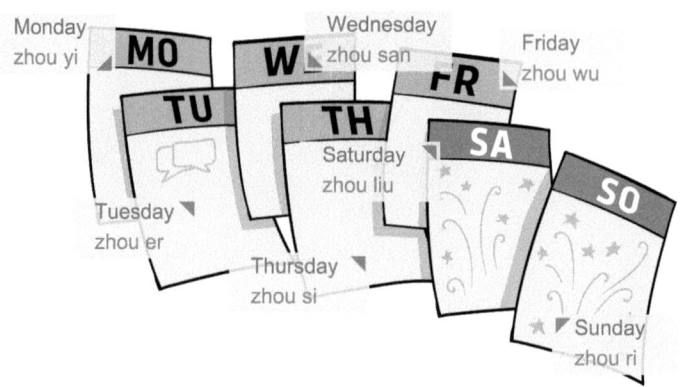

Monday
zhou yi

Tuesday
zhou er

Wednesday
zhou san

Thursday
zhou si

Friday
zhou wu

Saturday
zhou liu

Sunday
zhou ri

yesterday

zuo tian

today

jin tian

tomorrow

ming tian

morning

zao chen

noon

zhong wu

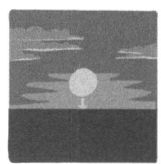

evening

wan shang

workdays

gong zuo ri

weekend

zhou mo

# year

## nian

rain
yu
spring
chun
summer
xia
wind
feng
fall
qiu
snow
xue
winter
dong


4.APRIL 11°
5.APRIL 4°
6.APRIL 13°
7.APRIL 8°
8.APRIL 10°


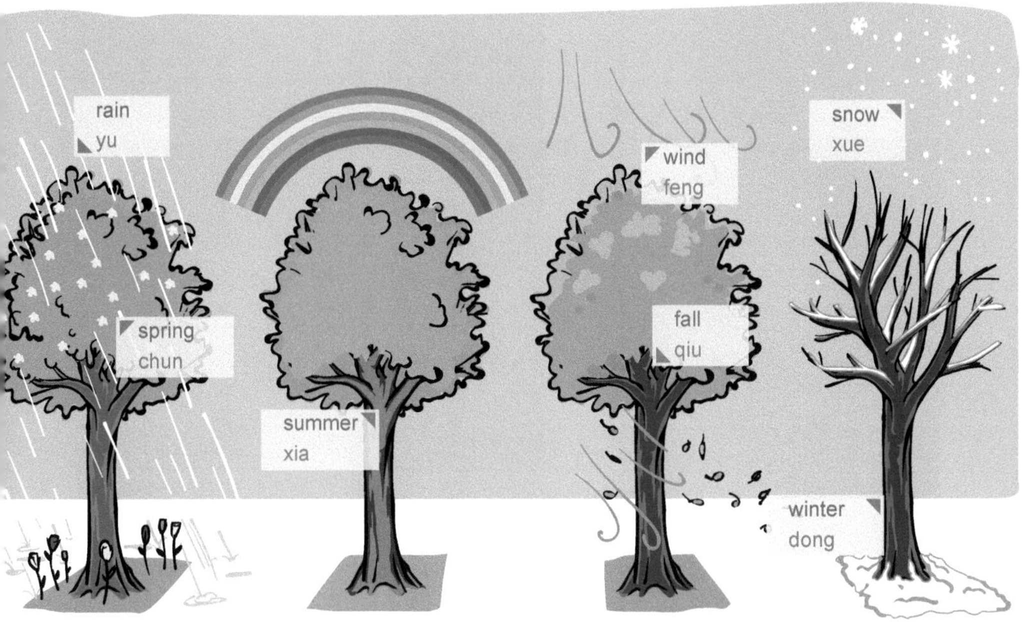

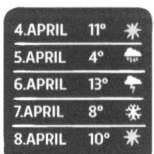

weather forecast

tian qi yu bao

F
C
120
90
60
30
0
-30
40
30
20
10
0
-10
-20


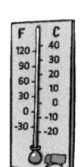

thermometer

wen du ji

sunshine

yang guang

cloud

yun

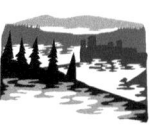

fog

wu

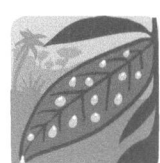

humidity

chao shi

lightning

shan dian

thunder

da lei

storm

feng bao

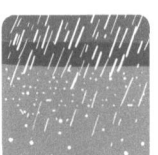

hail

bing bao

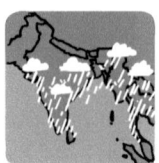

monsoon

ji feng

flood

hong shui

ice

bing

January

yi yue

February

er yue

March

san yue

April

si yue

May

wu yue

June

liu yue

July

qi yue

August

ba yue

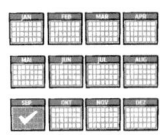

September
jiu yue

October
shi yue

November
shi yi yue

December
shi er yue

## shapes
## xing zhuang

circle
yuan xing

square
zheng fang xing

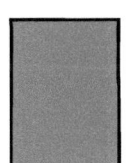

rectangle
chang fang xing

triangle
san jiao xing

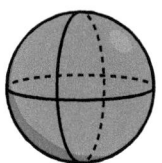

sphere
qiu ti

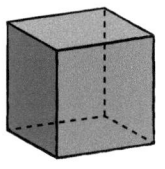

cube
li fang ti

# colors

white

bai

yellow

huang

orange

cheng

pink

fen

red

hong

purple

zi

blue

lan

green

lü

brown

zong

gray

hui

black

hei

a lot / a little

hen duo/shao xu

angry / calm

sheng qi/ping jing

beautiful / ugly

mei/chou

beginning / end

shou/wei

big / small

da/xiao

bright / dark

ming/an

brother / sister

xiong di/jie mei

clean / dirty

gan jing/ang zang

complete / incomplete

wan zheng/que shi

day / night

bai tian/wan shang

dead / alive

si/sheng

wide / narrow

kuan/zhai

**edible / inedible**

ke shi yong/fei shi yong

**evil / kind**

xie e/shan liang

**excited / bored**

xing fen/wu liao

**fat / thin**

pang/shou

**first / last**

di yi/zui hou

**friend / enemy**

peng you/di ren

**full / empty**

man/kong

**hard / soft**

ying/ruan

**heavy / light**

zhong/qing

**hunger / thirst**

e/ke

**ill / healthy**

sheng bing/jian kang

**illegal / legal**

fei fa/he fa

**intelligent / stupid**

cong ming/yu ben

**left / right**

zuo/you

**near / far**

jin/yuan

new / used

xin/jiu

nothing / something

mei you/you xie

old / young

lao/you

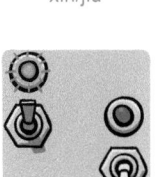

on / off

kai/guan

open / closed

da kai/he shang

quiet / loud

an jing/chao nao

rich / poor

fu/qiong

right / wrong

dui/cuo

rough / smooth

cu cao/guang hua

sad / happy

shang xin/gao xing

short / long

duan/chang

slow / fast

man/kuai

wet / dry

shi/gan

warm / cool

wen nuan/liang shuang

war / peace

zhan zheng/he ping

**0**

zero

ling

**1**

one

yi

**2**

two

er

**3**

three

san

**4**

four

si

**5**

five

wu

**6**

six

liu

**7**

seven

qi

**8**

eight

ba

**9**

nine

jiu

**10**

ten

shi

**11**

eleven

shi yi

**12**

twelve

shi er

**13**

thirteen

shi san

**14**

fourteen

shi si

**15**

fifteen

shi wu

**16**

sixteen

shi liu

**17**

seventeen

shi qi

**18**

eighteen

shi ba

**19**

nineteen

shi jiu

**20**

twenty

er shi

**100**

hundred

bai

**1.000**

thousand

qian

**1.000.000**

million

bai wan

English

ying yu

American English

mei shi ying yu

Chinese Mandarin

pu tong hua

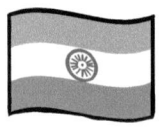

Hindi

yin di yu

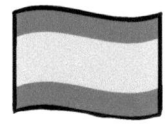

Spanish

xi ban ya yu

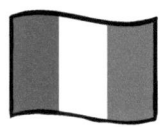

French

fa yu

Arabic

a la bo yu

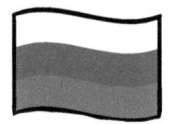

Russian

e yu

Portuguese

pu tao ya yu

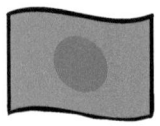

Bengali

feng jia la yu

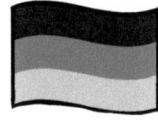

German

de yu

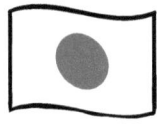

Japanese

ri yu

I
wo

you
ni

he / she / it
ta/ta/ta

we
wo men

you
ni men

they
ta men

who?
shei?

what?
shen me?

how?
zen yang?

where?
na li?

when?
shen me shi hou?

name
ming zi

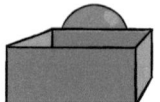

behind

hou mian

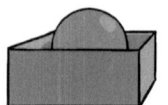

in

li mian

in front of

qian mian

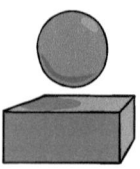

over

shang fang

on

shang mian

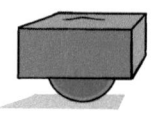

under

xia mian

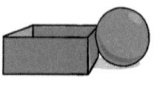

beside

pang bian

between

zhong jian

place

di dian